Extreme Weather
by Emma Rose

Table of Contents

Getting Started 2
Hurricane! 4
Tornado! 8
Blizzard! 12
Index 16

capstone
classroom

Getting Started

Weather. We talk about it often. "How warm is it today?" "Did you hear the thunderstorm last night?" "When is it going to rain?" "Have you ever seen so much snow?"

Weather affects your life every day. It helps you decide what to wear. Should you take an umbrella? Do you need an extra sweater? Weather affects what you do too. Will there be soccer practice if it rains?

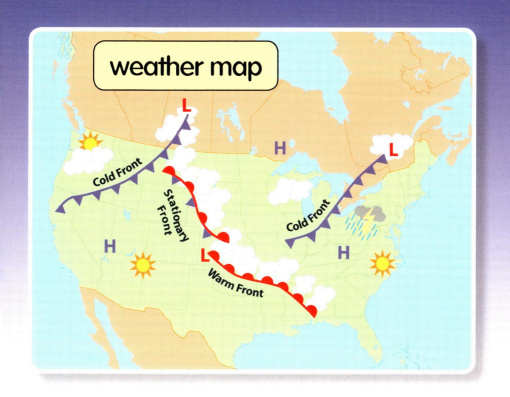

No matter where you live, your weather follows patterns. You may get rainy springs, hot summers, cool falls, and snowy winters. But when weather systems go wild, get ready for extreme weather.

Hurricane!

A hurricane is one of the most dangerous types of weather on Earth. It is a huge storm with heavy rains and very strong winds. Wind and rain swirl around a calm center, which is called the eye.

Hurricanes usually occur in the late summer or fall. Hurricanes often begin over an ocean. They often get stronger as they get closer to land.

Satellite pictures show the path that a hurricane follows. A meteorologist studies these satellite pictures. Meteorologists use these pictures to predict where and when a hurricane will reach the shore.

When a hurricane reaches land, strong winds can blow 75 to 190 miles per hour. That's strong enough to lift roofs off homes and knock down tall trees. Being outside in a hurricane is not safe.

Meteorologists give each hurricane a different boys' or girls' name. Hurricanes are named in order of the letters of the alphabet. The first hurricane of the year gets a name that starts with A. The next hurricane gets a name that starts with B, and so on.

For example, if the first hurricane of the year is named for a girl with the letter A, the next one will be given a boy's name starting with B, and so on.

Will they ever run out of names for hurricanes? No! That's because the same names are used every six years. If a hurricane is really big, its name might be "retired." Retired hurricane names, like Hurricane Katrina, won't ever be used again.

Tornado!

What other kind of storm is also very dangerous? A tornado! Tornadoes have very strong winds that twist around and around in a circle. Because of this, tornadoes are also called twisters.

Most tornadoes start as strong thunderstorms. But unlike hurricanes, tornadoes begin over land. A tornado reaches from the bottom of a thundercloud all the way down to the ground. A tornado is wider at the top than at the bottom, like an ice cream cone or a funnel. For this reason, tornadoes are also known as funnel clouds.

A tornado's winds can blow up to 300 miles per hour. That's strong enough to lift a house or a railroad car into the air and drop them down somewhere else.

Tornadoes strike in the United States more than in any other part of the world. They often happen in an area in the central part of the United States. This area's nickname is "Tornado Alley."

Tornadoes can happen any time of the year, but most strike between March and August. Meteorologists cannot predict tornadoes the way they can predict hurricanes. But they can let people know if a tornado is likely to occur. This is called a tornado watch. They can also warn people if a tornado is nearby. This is known as a tornado warning.

If there is a tornado warning, people need to know how to stay safe. They go into a safe room on a lower floor, such as a basement without windows. Then they don't need to worry about being hit by broken glass.

Blizzard!

Snow falls when there is moisture in the air and the temperature drops to the freezing point or below. Snow can be a pretty sight to see.

Sometimes snow can also be extreme. What happens when there is too much snow, too much wind, and very cold temperatures? The answer is a blizzard!

During a blizzard, the wind blows very hard. It's difficult to see through the snow. You may not be able to see much farther than the length of a football field. In a whiteout, you can't see anything but snow!

During a blizzard, winds create piles of snow called snowdrifts. Heavy snow and ice may pull down telephone wires or bury cars. It may be too dangerous to travel, so roads and airports may close. Schools and businesses may also close.

Blizzards, hurricanes, and tornadoes, are all very dangerous. You should stay inside during any of these storms. But when the storm is over, you might want to go to the library and find a book to learn more about it!

Index

blizzards, 12–15

eye (of hurricane), 4

funnel clouds, 8

hurricanes, 4–7, 11, 15

meteorologists, 5, 7, 11

names (of hurricanes), 7

rain, 2, 3, 4

satellite pictures, 5

snow, 2, 3, 12–15

thunderstorms, 2, 8

tornadoes, 8–11, 15

Tornado Alley, 10

twisters, 8

weather systems, 3

whiteout, 13

winds, 4, 6, 8, 9, 12, 13, 14